Deeper Woods

Michael Anderson

Copyright © 2017 Michael Anderson

All rights reserved.

ISBN-13: 978-1540892201

All Scripture is taken from the NASB version of the Bible unless otherwise noted.
"Scripture quotations taken from the New American Standard Bible® (NASB),
Copyright © 1960, 1962, 1963, 1968, 1971, 1972, 1973,
1975, 1977, 1995 by The Lockman Foundation
Used by permission. www.Lockman.org"

"Scripture quotations are from the ESV® Bible (The Holy Bible, English Standard Version®), copyright © 2001 by Crossway, a publishing ministry of Good News Publishers. Used by permission. All rights reserved."

Scriptures taken from the Holy Bible, New International Version®, NIV®. Copyright © 1973, 1978, 1984, 2011 by Biblica, Inc.™ Used by permission of Zondervan. All rights reserved worldwide. www.zondervan.com The "NIV" and "New International Version" are trademarks registered in the United States Patent and Trademark Office by Biblica, Inc.™

DEDICATION

To everyone who has ever pursued the passion of the call...

DEEPER WOODS

DEEPER WOODS

CONTENTS

Day 1	The Passion of the Pursuit	Pg. 10
Day 2	Expecting the Unexpected	Pg. 11
Day 3	Bird's Eye View	Pg. 13
Day 4	Time and Location	Pg. 14
Day 5	The Call	Pg. 15
Day 6	Trimming Back	Pg. 16
Day 7	The Secret	Pg. 17
Day 8	All Things	Pg. 18
Day 9	It is Better to Give Than Receive	Pg. 19
Day 10	God's-*GPS*	Pg. 21
Day 11	The Rescue	Pg. 22
Day 12	The Mission	Pg. 23
Day 13	Hope to the Hopeless	Pg. 25
Day 14	God's Will	Pg. 27
Day 15	Satan's Will	Pg. 28
Day 16	Trespass	Pg. 30
Day 17	The Harvest	Pg. 32
Day 18	The Fall	Pg. 33
Day 19	The Cross Hairs	Pg. 34
Day 20	Seeing the Unseen	Pg. 35

Day 21	The Man God Uses	Pg. 36
Day 22	A Friend Closer Than A Brother	Pg. 38
Day 23	Frustrating Circumstances	Pg. 39
Day 24	Persistence	Pg. 40
Day 25	Within Range	Pg. 41
Day 26	Faith That Works	Pg. 42
Day 27	Lessons Learned	Pg. 43
Day 28	The Investment	Pg. 45
Day 29	The Warden	Pg. 46
Day 30	The Right Way	Pg. 48
Day 31	The Final Hunt	Pg. 49

ACKNOWLEDGMENTS

Historian and Educator George Burton Adams said it best when he said, "There is no such thing as a 'self-made' man. We are made up of thousands of others."

To the countless *others;* I offer my sincere thanks *and* of appreciation. ~ Michael

A special thanks to all who made their contributions to this works end… Randy Hudson for his photography talents. Crystal Perry, Bobbie Faulkenberry and Cathy Lowes for their editorial labor. And to Peter Wing, Matt Scwhartz and Robert Mayfield for their pursuit tip contributions.

Nothing But Love For You Guys!

DEEPER WOODS
DAY 1

The Passion of the Pursuit

For those whom He foreknew, He also predestined to become conformed to the image of his Son, so that He would be the firstborn among many brethren;
Romans 8:29

Everyone who has ever experienced the passion of what it means to pursue the whitetail, can relate to the pursuit itself. It will drive you to get up before dawn in the midst of frosty temperatures, trek unfavorable terrain, sweat the climb in what is known to be a sweet spot and travel corridor for the big bucks in the area. The passion of the pursuit will drive every hunter to do and act in ways that would seem insane to those who have not experienced its call. It is in this passion, that we who call ourselves hunters will gladly pursue the chance to lay hands on a trophy harvest. It is a feeling that is hard to verbalize, but that every hunter can relate to - it is the passion of the pursuit.

Why is this? Why is it that we feel driven to keep pressing on in this passion? I would submit it lies within the way God has wired us as men and women, created in His image.

While many of us identify this pursuit with hopes of that next wall hanger, God has also called us as a part of his creation, a pursuit to be conformed to His image. What does this mean, you may ask? It means that God has an awesome desire for us to pursue the passion of becoming a trophy of His grace. To walk, talk and embody the very person of Jesus through every move we make by His enabling Spirit residing on the inside of us. We demonstrate this when we are willing to suffer for the betterment of our families, churches and fellow man. It means that His practical kindness is seen manifested in the way we hunt, love and serve. In essence, it is seen when we pursue the things of the Kingdom to come rather than the kingdoms of this world. Only when we possess the passion of this pursuit, do we truly begin to experience life and life more abundantly.

Pursuit Tip

Consider your entry points and stand locations. When possible try to avoid entry through bedding areas that can bump the deer before they get to their feet.

DEEPER WOODS
DAY 2

Expecting the Unexpected

...but sanctify Christ as Lord in your hearts, always being ready to make a defense to everyone who asks you to give an account for the hope that is in you, yet with gentleness and reverence,
1 Peter 3:15

I remember it like it was yesterday. I was coming home on the back road that parallels my house and provides a back driveway. As I approached my driveway, there he was, The Man! He was a beautiful stud of a deer standing with beautiful symmetries on his rack, postured in that confidence only dominant bucks exude. He was headed in the direction where I just moved my climber on the outskirts of some oak trees that were dropping acorns by the bucket full. My theory was he was headed that way to feed for the night and likely would bed down close by, placing him in the neighborhood the next morning.

The stalk began at 5 the next morning. I took the scent shower, got dressed and headed down the road with bow in hand. Approaching my climber, I tied twine to it as a pull-up rope. After five good climbs up the tree, the twine worked its way out of my pocket falling to the ground. So, down I go. Ten climbs up on the ascending trek the twine got tight, so I began to pull the bow up. Suddenly, the twine snapped sending the bow hurling to the ground. If you have ever experienced this, you can relate to the mounting pain, rising blood pressure and frustration. So back down I go again to attach the bow to the back clip of my harness, and then finally I make it back up the tree with all equipment in tow. By this point, I am convinced that every deer within ten miles has crossed county lines. I had nearly dismissed the notion at this point of trying to be quiet to the point that the ripping of bark sounded like a saw mill. Surely if that wasn't enough to drive the deer away, the clanging of bow to climber as it swayed on my back from side to side would seal the deal.

Finally, I was able to settle in precisely at the break of dawn. With just enough time to pull my release out of my pocket and secure my cellphone, I noticed the silhouette of a deer approximately thirty yards out. The scarcity of light left me unable to locate it with the range finder, so I went ahead and stood up. As I got to my feet, I saw he was walking and feeding straight towards me giving me little time to even think. Now only fifteen yards directly in front of me, he looked up and it was him, The Man!

Certain he was looking at me and knowing at any minute he was poised to jet out of there, to my surprise he didn't. He began walking to my left while I'm desperately trying to get the release attached. By this time, to say buck fever had kicked in was an understatement, thus creating a challenge to attach the release to the string. Finally successful, I drew back taking aim with him now only steps from retreating behind the vines that were cascading from the trees. I quickly called out, catching his attention and freezing him in his tracks. He threw his head around and the motion revealed the weight of his rack. Releasing my shot, I anxiously watched as the nocturnal arrow zipped high over his back, while he ran off never to be seen again.

Wow, what a hunt! Even in the midst of severe disappointment, I still look back at that hunt with excitement. I can't tell you how many times I have replayed those events over in my mind, wondering what I should have done differently.

One conclusion I reached - we should always expect the unexpected. Considering the circumstances, I truly didn't expect to have that encounter with that buck the way I did. This experience also reminded me of when Peter told the Church in 1 Peter 3:15, "...but sanctify Christ as Lord in your hearts, always being ready to make a defense to everyone who asks you to give an account for the hope that is in you, yet with gentleness and reverence,". He was reminding them that as believers, we are always to carry the message of Christ with us wherever we go. In essence, we are to expect the unexpected opportunities Christ presents us to deliver a shot of His grace, love and mercy into the hearts of those who cross our path. To the club, to the range or on our jobs we are always to be ready in season and out of season. We should speak of the cause and testimony of Christ in our lives to those around us, even to those we may not have expected to come walking our way!

Pursuit Tip
All woods are not the same. Food, water and shelter are three primary items that deer seek. Find these three ingredients in close proximity of each other, and there you will find your deer.

DEEPER WOODS
DAY 3

Bird's Eye View

Two are better than one because they have a good return for their labor. For if either of them falls, the one will lift up his companion. But woe to the one who falls when there is not another to lift his up.
Ecclesiastes 4:9-10

There is double the excitement when hunting with a partner. Not only do the odds of your potential success increase from just hunting solo, you now double your chances to taste the thrill through your friend's experiences.

One early season hunt, I remember being in a stand situated on the edge of the property line with shooting lanes looking to the left, right and in front of me. Deer movement had been excellent that morning. Looking to my left at the end of the lane slightly behind the limbs, I saw what looked to be a nice buck. I exhausted every call in my bag of tricks except hollering the deer's name to COME! At this point is where the bad news and good news unfolded. The bad news was the buck finally committed to walk away from my wooing, but the good news was he was headed directly to my buddy's stand 300 yards away! Knowing that I had dripped drops of Tinks 69 on the trail and direction he was headed, added to the excitement. My phone was quickly sending the text saying, "shooter buck coming your way!" Sure enough after seven or eight minutes, BOOM! The ringing of the 7mm rang out! Though the six point was not a wall hanger, it sure made for a thrilling hunt and harvest and one that having the "bird's eye view" proved to be a contributing factor.

How about you? Have you ever had the advantage of having someone give information that you didn't have access to or couldn't see coming that played to your advantage? The Bible says in Ecclesiastes 4:9-10 "Two are better than one because they have a good return for their labor. For if either of them falls, the one will lift up his companion. But woe to the one who falls when there is not another to lift his up." We all have the built-in nature to act independently. When we open up our lives to allow friends, co-workers and brothers and sisters in Christ access into our hearts, they can provide intel that we simply cannot see for ourselves. By doing so, our potential for success in life can rise. Only when we walk humbly and are submissive enough to receive accountability for all areas of our lives, are we then able to take a step closer to living out the Victorious Christian Life. We then become all that God has designed for us to be in Christ.

Pursuit Tip
Try hunting the woods with a friend as much as possible. This not only provides safety measures but also can help with the chances of calling deer in.

DEEPER WOODS
DAY 4

Time and Location

Jesus answered and said to him, "Truly, truly, I say to you, unless one is born again he cannot see the kingdom of God." John 3:3

Do you remember your first hunt? How about your first kill? Boy, I sure do. I can tell you what was happening right before he stepped out, the location it occurred, the size of the deer and so forth. There is something about that first time we smoked that first whitetail that has a lasting impression in our memory.

The same should ring true for our spiritual lives. The day we experienced the grace of Jesus should be a moment we never forget. Jesus told a man by the name of Nicodemus in John 3, that unless a man be born again, he will not inherit the kingdom of heaven. Here's what we know to be true about all physical births, and when new life enters this world; there is always a definite time, place and change that occurs as a result of it. The same is true for the spiritual birth. We can parallel the detailed memory recall of our first deer to that of our spiritual birthdays. While some of the details may not be as clear as others, there should be no doubt to the time, place and location of when Jesus climbed into the stand of our hearts.

I have heard many reference that they have, "always been a 'Christian'," perhaps because they were raised in a Christian home or taken to church from a very young age. However, nothing could be further from the truth. Meaning, there has to come the time in everyone's life that we acknowledge for ourselves we have missed the bull's eye of God's standard of perfection. We have broken God's moral laws found within the Ten Commandments.

By faith, we choose to believe that Jesus is God's only Son who died for our sins on the cross and was raised back to life on the third day on our behalf. By faith, we receive this life-changing transformation in our lives. When we do this, it becomes a day we never forget. It becomes when everything begins to take on a whole new meaning for the first time. *the time*

Pursuit Tip
A deer's number one weapon against predators is its nose. Defeat this in a whitetail and your chances of success can rise drastically.

DEEPER WOODS
DAY 5

The Call

My sheep hear My voice, and I know them, and they follow Me; and I give eternal life to them, and they will never perish; and no one will snatch them out of My hand.
John 10:27-28

I can remember watching a small six point step out one morning, looking as if he was trailing does who had recently passed that way. He quickly cut the corner preventing me from getting a decent look. After rounding the bend and vanishing out of sight, I quickly hit my Primo's buck roar. To my excitement, he turned completely around, came trotting back in, thus allowing me a better look. This second look ultimately allowed me to decide to give him a pass to potentially grow.

Nothing compares to seeing a deer come prancing in to a bleat call or circling back to a grunt call. There is a thrill about being able to manipulate wild game this way that evokes a feeling of mastery over the mysterious whitetail. Because deer know and recognize these calls as a part of their own language and lingo, they respond. Similarly, I have learned over the course of my seventeen years as a Christ follower, that there are primary ways in which God speaks and calls to His creation, specifically you and I.

They are:
- His Word
- His People
- His Creation

God's Word is the best application for us to hear God's call and will for our everyday lives. He uses His people who are walking in accordance to His word to offer us exhortation and guidance. And, He also gives us a revelation of Himself through His creation as a clear call of making Himself known to us.

Jesus said in John's gospel 10:27, "My sheep hear My voice, and I know them, and they follow Me." One thing is clear from this teaching; those who know Jesus, know His voice, and His voice, they follow. What a great truth to know that the Creator still calls and speaks to His creation. What perhaps do you hear God calling you to respond to today?

Pursuit Tip

Game calls are a great addition to increasing one's chances of seeing deer. Consider investing in a grunt, snort wheeze, rattle or bleat call and experiment with them. Be mesmerized when they actually work!

DEEPER WOODS
DAY 6

Trimming Back

I am the true vine, and my Father is the gardener. He cuts off every branch in me that bears no fruit, while every branch that does bear fruit he prunes so that it will be even more fruitful.
John 15:1-3 (NIV)

Hunters know all to well that at some point it will be necessary that they and a blade will become familiar friends. Whether in the form of a chainsaw, pole saw or any other type of saw, this relationship becomes a must when considering trimming up stands and thickets for producing shooting lanes. Sometimes this process can be a painstakingly, sweaty affair exposing endless work with each section cleared. Other times it only takes one or two carefully considered limbs that open up just the right view you were looking for, providing that best chance of successfully getting off a clean shot.

Jesus was the master of parables, which is the art of taking an earthly story and giving it a heavenly meaning for the people of His day and time. On one occasion, He told those listening, "I am the true vine, and my Father is the gardener. He cuts off every branch in me that bears no fruit, while every branch that does bear fruit He prunes so that they will be even more fruitful" (John 15 1-3). Jesus was pointing out that there are two types of people. One are those who disobey His teachings and are cut off never to be useful again, remaining separated from His presence for eternity. Second are those who belong to Him; those who walk with Him, talk with his and follow his commands in loving obedience. Jesus tell us that it is in the lives of these followers that Christ trims back areas of their lives with His undeserving favor. Attitudes, habits and vices are all areas that the Father prunes out of our lives in order to shape and mold us into the people He desires for us to be.

As painful as the trimming process can be to expose a shooting lane, the same can be said when we submit to the rhythm of the Father's grace of pruning in our lives. We can be assured that the end result will lead the world to seeing a clear reflection of our lives that is a straight lane leading to the prize and person of Christ Jesus!

Pursuit Tip

Consider less as more when trimming lanes, especially in thicker wooded locations. Deer know their habitats well and notice change. Consider trimming out only what is necessary for producing the best shot possible. Over pruning could run the risk of knocking deer off their natural travel corridors.

DEEPER WOODS
DAY 7

The Secret

I know what it is to be in need, and I know what it is to have plenty. I have learned the secret of being content in any and every situation, whether well fed or hungry, whether living in plenty or in want.
Philippians 4:12 (NIV)

Whether I'm running late to the stand on one of the best weather mornings of the year, in almost the dead of rut, or on the days I haven't put eyes on the big boy I've been chasing through the season, nor seen a single deer after countless hours of sitting, God gently reminds me of the great privilege that simply goes with the process. The process of being able to be a part of such a wonderful sport and partaking in His great outdoors is such a tremendous blessing.

In the sport of hunting or the game of life itself, it is very easy to draw the card of discontentment when things do not go quite the way we would hope. This is where Paul's life experience and words serve as a reminder to us all when he wrote, "I know what it is to be in need, and I know what it is to have plenty. I have learned the secret of being content in any and every situation, whether well fed or hungry, whether living in plenty or in want (Philippians 4:12 *NIV*)." Like hunting, life has ways that get us down and discouraged from focusing on the things we don't have rather than the blessings we do have, if we allow it.

So let this truth remind us all! Enjoy the process of seeking a life of contentment filled with the enjoyment of the blessings we all have been afforded ---especially when pursuing the passion of the game we all know as hunting!

Pursuit Tip

On especially cold winter mornings, pick up a pair of wool socks. Before putting them on try wearing a thin, what I like to call pair of church socks, underneath. This will help keep your feet from sweating and provide warmth through the hunt!

DEEPER WOODS
DAY 8

All Things

in everything give thanks; for this is God's will for you in Christ Jesus.
I Thessalonians 5:18

Few things are as exhilarating as staring a whitetail eyeball to eyeball at eleven yards and being able to thank the Lord for the experience in the middle of the intensity. During this stand down, you never know if at any second he's going to jet out of dodge or if the stealthy stalk is going to payoff. If you have spent any significant time in the field, it's almost a sure fire bet that you too have experienced the highest of highs and the lowest of lows. Often I have seen guys post on social media after a harvest, especially of a nice buck, things like, "God is good, the Lord blessed me" and so forth. While there is certainly nothing wrong with the sentiment, I have often found myself wondering, does God change when the buck of a lifetime gets missed or when the all common scenarios of getting busted occurs? The obvious answer to our rhetorical question--absolutely not!

We need to learn to master our responses with an attitude of gratitude in all phases of life's circumstances. This is possible regardless of whether our current circumstances are made up of the good, bad or ugly events that occur throughout life and hunting. We can be assured that when we give thanks in all things, we are fulfilling an intricate piece of God's will for our lives.

When we kill, we praise Him; and when we don't, we still praise Him!

Pursuit Tip
Use the layout of the land to really hone in on how the deer travel. Funnels, pinch points or bottle necks are keys to look for to increase the chances towards the harvest.

DEEPER WOODS
DAY 9

It is Better to Give than to Receive

In everything I showed you that by working hard in this manner you must help the weak and remember the words of the Lord Jesus, that He Himself said, 'It is more blessed to give than to receive.'
Acts 20:35

It was the prime time of the year when a buddy from out of state journeyed down for a two day hunt. On the evening of the first hunt, we were headed to a popular power line stand that always has frequent deer movement through the course of the season. A few days before his arrival, I added a little extra corn to his hunting spot.

Anticipation was building on the ride over. We were busy deliberating deer traffic patterns around the stand and possible kill shot yardage he could expect. In the midst of the calculations, he casually referenced he would be hunting with his shotgun. I quickly dismissed this comment as his attempt at humor. Power line and shotgun? Yeah, right!

Shortly after directing him to his stand and settling in at mine, the deer activity began. Wasting no time, I reported the activity via text, and he responded with, "I do too!" "He does too", I thought? What in the world? I knew he had made a special trip to get doe tags, and he is telling me he sees deer and yet I have heard no shot. On top of this, I know for a fact he was very anxious to pull the trigger, as we had discussed he would take the first opportunity. I quickly text him back asking the status. He responds with saying the deer was seventy yards out! Oh my goodness! Your kidding me right ?! He really did have a shotgun! I told my buddy you better text your wife and tell her you have to go to Wal-Mart because you've got to buy a rifle tonight! Needless to say, he did not get a shot that evening.

As morning two of the hunt dawned, I revealed the plan. I was going to give him my rifle and move him to another stand location proven worthy for morning hunts. I would take my bow and get positioned shortly behind him. I must admit, I've never given my personal gun to anyone to hunt with before. Besides, a hunter's weapon is like his dog -- it's his best friend that holds a special place in the heart!

The morning was perfect! Wind was at minimum; an icy frost covered the ground, glowing in the bright sunshine. We were close enough to hear each others' grunt calls. At approximately 8:15, I shot him a text to tell him it was almost primetime for potential deer movement. Within fifteen minutes, one of the coolest things I have ever experienced while hunting occurred. I heard my buddy make the familiar goat sound, 'bahhing'. It's the call we often use to get a deer to freeze or look our direction right before a shot is unloaded. Well, that's exactly what happened as the 30-06 shuddered across the pasture! In no time, we were down from our stands to trail the eight pointer he had just shot!
While I certainly did not predict how this unfolded, this experience by far

rises to the top of the hundreds of hunts I've enjoyed. The joy that still stems from that hunt, I believe, is rooted in the principle that the Giver of all good things provides. The principle that it is always more blessed to give than to receive rings true. We live in a world of give me, give me, give me! There is the mentality of me first, instead of putting others first. Our world needs more selfless people willing to put their desires and likes secondary, while elevating others to being primary. On that chilly morning, I was reminded convincingly that it truly is more blessed to give than it is to receive. This hunt demonstrates that giving can be wrapped in the most exceptional ways!

Life is at its best when it is given away.

Pursuit Tip
There are usually a few 'perfect' days in every season, when every deer in the woods is on their feet. The most ideal hunting conditions can come when temperatures are low and the barometer is high.

DEEPER WOODS
DAY 10

God's GPS

For I am convinced that neither death, nor life, nor angels, nor principalities, nor things present, nor things to come, nor powers, nor height, nor depth, nor any other created thing, will be able to separate us from the love of God, which is in Christ Jesus our Lord.
Romans 8:38-39

One of the safety tactics I began using while hunting is the sharing location feature iMessage on my iPhone. This feature allows me to share my location at all times with friends as long as I have a signal available. Whether I'm in an easily accessible location or in the climber off the beaten path, someone has knowledge of my whereabouts at all times. This is especially valuable in should an accident occur.

Global Positioning Systems (GPS) are a phenomenon that has taken technology and even hunting to a whole new level over the last few years. This technology allows for one's whereabouts and stand locations to be easily accessible at all times. Just like the technological GPS, GPSs can also serve as a reminder of God's sovereignty and omniscience in our lives.

The word omniscient simply means, "knowing everything or having unlimited understanding or knowledge." Whether it is the day you were born, the day you will die or 'the dash' in between that represents all the days of your life, nothing is beyond the grasp of God's knowledge. There is a wonderful concept about God's knowledge of us, whether we feel great or shamefully secretive. We can rest assured in the fact that God's love for us never changes! In fact, God's GPS, *God's Plan of Salvation,* in the form of Him sending his one and only Son into this world to take our sins through His death on the cross and resurrection from the grave, was demonstrated to us all! Because He knows all, He also is able to forgive all. It is in this truth we can cling to and trust in His GPS for our lives through total faith in His Son the Lord Jesus Christ!

Pursuit Tip

Downloading apps that show land layouts and wind directions can be a great tool. Use for considering where to best place a stand or deciding which stand to hunt depending on wind direction on any given day.

DEEPER WOODS
DAY 11

The Rescue

For he has rescued us from the dominion of darkness and brought us into the kingdom of the Son he loves
Colossians 1:13 (NIV)

Five years ago I was given a full-blooded, rescue boxer. Her name is Layla. She was rescued from an abusive situation and placed in an adoption program for dogs like herself.

Naturally, as I would hang stands, check cameras and plant food plots, Layla would tag along in the background. She often would go out in front exploring the honey holes with me. On one particular hunt, I shot a deer near my house and felt confident the shot was good. However, the retrieval was not. Daylight was fading and the woods quickly became dark. After going back to the house to get my vehicle for added light, I decided to let Layla tag along.

Given Layla's breed and background, I was not expecting what happened that day. As I was searching, Layla wandered off on her own and led me right to the prize! I don't know who was more excited, me or her. Four years have past since my discovery, and I cannot tell you the joy she has brought when it comes to her knack for trailing deer. Now my buddies know -- if they have blood – that I have a dog!

Layla's background reminds me how God works in our lives. He rescues us from an abusive situation marked with wounds and scars from our past, adopts us into His family of grace and gives us a purpose we never knew before. The Bible describes it like this, "For He rescued us from the domain of darkness, and transferred us to the kingdom of his beloved Son," (Colossians 1:13-14 NIV). Because God has rescued us, He desires to use us. We can be confident that He wants to use our time, talent and treasures to display His majesty and glory to a watching world that extends to the ends of the earth. When we allow Him to have His will and way in us, He then is able to display the rescue of His grace through us!

Pursuit Tip

Soil testing can be a vital ingredient to learning the proper nutrients needed before planting a food plot. Check with your local lawn and gardening store to see if they offer soil sample testing, as some do.

DEEPER WOODS
DAY 12

The Mission

All authority in heaven and on earth has been given to me. Therefore go and make disciples of all nations, baptizing them in the name of the Father and of the Son and of the Holy Spirit, and teaching them to obey everything I have commanded you. And surely I am with you always, to the very end of the age.
Matthew 28:18-20(NIV)

Though all hunts, set ups and scenarios differ, one constant remains -- the mission! Some are a smooth sneak into a pasture stand that allows for ease and comfort of the hunt. Yet some are a trek into the deeper woods, where mastering the mechanics of each carefully placed step determines secrecy and stealth to circumvent rustling of leaves and the cracking of fallen branches. All – out effort to see the mission of the harvest accomplished! The sacrifices we as hunters will endure to see this mission to it's end is amazing.

Do you know what amazes me? The parallel between the traits of the whitetail hunter and the person the modern church calls a missionary. Both are on a mission. Both groups are made up of the toughest, grittiest and determined men and women on the planet.

Journey with me. Missionaries travel long and far to see the mission of Jesus Christ proclaimed and carried out. In the same way, there is no extent a hunter will not journey to see the mission of the hunt carried out. Missionaries sacrifice out of their treasuries to ensure proper supplies and equipment are in place to better serve the mission. Likewise, the hunter will invest in weaponries, modification upgrades, trail cameras and the like just to feel an edge in the field.

Jesus said in Matthew 28:16-18, "And Jesus came up and spoke to them, saying, 'All authority has been given to Me in heaven and on earth. Go therefore and make disciples of all the nations, baptizing them in the name of the Father and the Son and the Holy Spirit, teaching them to observe all that I commanded you; and lo, I am with you always, even to the end of the age (NIV).'" A few important words jump out for those of us who desire to go deeper in our walk with Christ. Did you notice that Jesus said "go"! The verb tense being used here is not referring to a one time event of 'going'. It actually is best translated, *"as you are going."*

Question! When the master speaks, does the servant have an option of obeying? As potential followers of Christ, the command of going into all nations is not a secondary option to be considered, but a mandated priority to be embraced. Secondly, notice the objective of the mission is to make disciples. A disciple is someone who learns to follow the ways of another. Just like many of you perhaps have passed on the legacy and tips of the trade of hunting to the younger generation, Christ calls us to do the same when it comes to passing his teachings on to others.

DEEPER WOODS

To many this call and command may seem like a foreign trail to follow. For those who desire complete surrender to the call and mission of Christ, it is the obvious embrace needed. Consider this year taking 1% of your time -- approximately 1 week out of 365 days – and spend it serving Christ in another context outside of your own. Conduct a ministry outreach with your church by journeying to a low income housing development or jump on a plane and experience serving Christ in a third world country. For the Christ follower, our command is both near and far and nothing is greater than being on mission for Christ.

Pursuit Tip

Rubber boots are the best option when trying to remain scent free. Leather and other materials absorb odors that in return the deer can smell, tipping them off to danger.

DEEPER WOODS
DAY 13

Hope To the Hopeless

But now, Lord, what do I look for?
My hope is in you.
Psalm 39:7 (NIV)

It was Christmas morning. My sisters and nephews live three hours towards the coast in Charleston, SC. Since we were not gathering until lunchtime, I had time for a late season early morning hunt. Not all, but most rut activity in this part of the South, has ceased. The buck sightings become few and far between, and one can only hope for a late season slip up on their part.

I decided to hunt what I call the fireman stand. Several years ago, the woods caught fire in that area, burning a section between a tract of pines, which made for a great food plot area. Some nice bucks had been caught on camera through the season. Although I had hunted here numerous times through the season, I had honestly never spotted a single deer, which was not the norm for this stand location. As I was sitting there playing on my phone, I noticed a doe come into view. Having already tagged out, with excitement I simply admired the beauty and elegance in God's creature..

Suddenly, out of nowhere she jets out of there! Nearly certain she didn't know I was anywhere around, I was puzzled at her behavior. Then abruptly, a buck comes nervously pursuing! Startled in unbelief, I immediately begin easing the rifle to the rail of the tripod. By the time I could get the gun up, he had already crossed out of sight. As I waited to see what might happen next, she popped back out in the corn pile. This had all the signs that he would be next! Sure enough he did, allowing me just enough time to get a visual of his rack telling me he was right at the ears. Not the bigger ones in the region, but certainly delightful enough to know if he stepped back out, we would unwrap the gift presenting itself under the tree on this Christmas morning! After a few minutes passed, he came back out for the third time. Only this time, the Remington and Nikon were locked and ready!

God blessed me that Christmas morning with an awesome hope-filled hunt and harvest that will never soon be forgotten. From that hunt forward, I will always possess the hope, that regardless of the circumstances or timing of the season, there is always hope even when there seems to be none of harvesting a late season buck.

Hope is a powerful force in this world. It is what puts the wind in our sails for the chance of a better tomorrow. There is nothing more inspiring that gives reason for hope in the darkest of days we may ever face, than that hope which comes from God.

The letter written to the church in Rome expresses this well when Paul wrote, "Rejoice in hope, be patient in tribulation, be constant in prayer (Romans 12:12 ESV)." In this life we are promised as followers of Jesus that we will face tribulations. The awesome news that follows this is that we too are also able to rejoice when we possess hope, in what otherwise would seem like a hopeless situation.

Perhaps this day you are going through the unthinkable. Perhaps your hope has seemingly run out. May you be reminded that regardless of the circumstances or season of life you are walking in, that hope has a Name and His Name is Jesus!

Pursuit Tip

Baking soda makes for a great inexpensive way to wash hunting clothes while eliminating scent.

DEEPER WOODS
DAY 14

God's Will

He has told you, O man, what is good; And what does the Lord require of you? But to do justice, to love kindness, and to walk humbly with your God.
Micah 6:8

One of the recent phenomenons that has revolutionized hunting is the trail camera. Every time we capture a nice buck cruising the area, it is like Christmas morning! This is also a useful tool to study the herd on a property, and it heightens the excitement of knowing at any second what may step out! Peering into this world is also a great mystery. Sometimes certain deer only seem to show up at night. When this happens, the guessing game begins! More times than I care to recall, I have wondered if I will ever get a chance to witness from my stand the images captured on camera.

Many times, God's will can leave us with similar feelings. Feelings of wondering what does He want and desire of me? God's written and inspired Word helps provide a clear picture of helping answer that question. The Old Testament prophet Micah wrote, *"He has told you, O man, what is good; And what does the Lord require of you? But to do justice, to love kindness, and to walk humbly with your God"* (Micah 6:8).

Justice is executing that which is right. Kindness shows up in the form of being friendly, generous, and considerate. And boy have I met some hunters that could use a good dose of that! Humility is acknowledging the source of all we have or ever hope to have and accomplish is from the hand of Almighty God and not ourselves.

Though God may seem distant at times, His will for our lives can be known. This begins by pursuing the things that reflect His character and then demonstrating those traits to everyone who crosses our path. When, by His grace, we reflect justice, kindness and humility, we are then providing a picture perfect reflection to the world of the Father's will for our lives.

Pursuit Tip

When positioning trail cameras, consider placing them on well worn travel areas to enhance your chances of getting frequent pictures.

DEEPER WOODS
DAY 15

Satan's Will

The thief comes only to steal and kill and destroy; I came that they may have life, and have it abundantly.
John 10:10

Mid-season one afternoon, a newly discovered scrape was found near a new spot overlooking a creek bank. Not having the time to hang a new stand and run the risk of spooking the deer from trimming out shooting lanes, I perched on the ground with my Daddy's Winchester 30-30 in hand, waiting it out. Not long into the hunt, I had three large doe charge from the vicinity of the scrape. The hunt was on!

I have to say their behavior was very strange. For nearly five minutes they all froze, not even taking a single step. My thought was, big boy is coming! Then without warning, they suddenly seem to be motivated to disappear with quickness, and I mean quick! Taken off-guard, I continued to sit on the frigid ground waiting it out. Fifteen minutes later, I would witness one of the wildest encounters I believe I have ever seen.

Two seemingly small deer flashed on the scene. I knew the buck wasn't far! Sure enough there he came! However, there was one BIG problem. What I thought were small does, were actually two coyotes in pursuit of the buck. Unable to get a clean shot, the only thing I could do was watch it unfold.

The crisp splash from the buck's leap into the creek echoed through the woods. The coyotes followed suit. I watched in awe as the buck rushed the coyotes through debris and limbs up on the creek bank, like a bull fight. It was incredible to say the least. The coyotes departed and the buck maintained his position wading in the water for another six or seven minutes. It was truly unlike anything I have ever witnessed.

There's an article in the **Grandview Outdoors** on how coyotes affect whitetail deer. In this article, the author makes reference to a six year study, using tracking collars, that took place in the Southeast pertaining to interactions between coyotes and whitetail deer. It states, "If the collar stopped moving for a set period of time, indicating the fawn had died, researchers went to the site and determined the cause of mortality. The results were astounding. Researchers involved in the study, which took place on the grounds of the Savannah River nuclear facility site, knew coyotes ate deer fawns. They had no idea they ate so many. As it turned out, 80 percent of the fawns that died from all causes were killed by coyotes ("How coyotes affect deer." *Grand View Outdoors*, http://www.grandviewoutdoors.com/big-game-hunting/how-coyotes-affect-deer/ Accessed 3 Feb. 2017)." If you talk to enough hunters, it does not take long to get a consensus that predators are a tremendous contributor to the decrease in whitetails across the country. Likewise, there is a stark comparison of the whitetail predator to the predator of our souls, namely that of Satan--Lucifer, the serpent of old.

The Bible describes him as more cunning and crafty than all the other beasts of the field. (Genesis 3) And just as God has a perfect will for our lives, this predator has an imperfect one. His will is to kill, destroy and control our future as part of his plan. There is one thing we should all note about this killer--the Bible also asserts that Satan's will is rarely packaged in the form of blatant evil. More often, it is subtly presented as pleasing to the eye, satisfying towards the boastful pride of life and all it's evil desires. In fact, we learn in 2 Corinthians 11:14 that Satan disguises himself as an angel of light. Extra marital affairs and gambling, just to name a couple, have their attractive lure. However, we can all be assured that no matter how pretty the picture Satan may paint for us, his chief desire for our lives is to kill, steal and destroy them, both physically and spiritually. The best choice for us is to always prayerfully be on the lookout for his predatory attacks knowing that, "He who is in you is greater than he who is in the world" (1 John 4:4 ESV)."

Pursuit Tip

Do not call it quits on a potential hunt just because you may be running late. Like the saying goes, you can't kill them at the house!

DEEPER WOODS
DAY 16

Trespass

For all have sinned and fall short of the glory of God
Romans 3:23

ALL deer are always 100 yards across the property line, right?! I had just obtained permission to hunt a brand new track of land that I just knew would be perfect! So the prepping began. I begin scouting the layout of the land using Google Earth and placed a camera in a key travel corridor for the deer. In the mean time, I learned the property line did not extend to where my camera location was set up. Thankfully, due to some good friends, I was able to begin the process of gaining permission to hunt the adjoining property. However, there would be about a week process for that to finalize. In the meantime, I waited.

In the waiting period, I decided to check the camera just to see if any deer had been frequenting the area. And would you believe -- it, one of the most awesome deer I had ever captured to date was caught cheesing for the camera in broad daylight! "Holy Cow" is what I said! Check him out on the left! I hardly could contain my excitement, but it was tempered with the agony of knowing I had not gained permission as of yet to hunt him. What do I do? Hunt him and potentially kill him by trespassing, or should I wait in hopes he strolls the neighborhood in a week or so.

I'm certain this is a dilemma every hunter reading this has faced in the history of their hunting career. At some point I think every hunter believes the *good* deer are *always* right across the property line, aren't they, lol?

As I look back on that event, I am reminded of how enticing is the forbidden call. The call will rationalize whispers of compromise. One look won't hurt my marriage; one taste won't hurt anyone; or one lapse in integrity won't be detrimental to my career. If I have learned anything in the game of life it's this--the vices and sins of this world, regardless of the outward measure of impact, are always appealing to the lust of the eye and to the boastful pride of man. In the end, it deceives us into believing that the lure will make our lives better.

Satan told Adam and Eve this same lie in the Garden of Eden: eat of the forbidden fruit and you will become like God, knowing the difference between good and evil. Friends, let me stop and say, there is nothing good about knowing evil. However, this concept and the lure of the fruit's beauty enticed the two of them to fall victim to disobeying God's command, bringing about its consequences of separation from God in the form of death for all mankind. The Bible says there is pleasure in sin for a season.

I could have stalked that monster hard and heavy and perhaps even put him on my wall for all to see. Great pleasure would have followed and a sense of accomplishment...for a season. Thankfully, I thought about having to answer the question of where I killed the deer. My answer would be a sad reminder of my disobedience as a child of God. It has been said that integrity is doing what is right even when no one is looking. May we be reminded that whether we work, hunt or play, we always do so with an audience of One in view.

Pursuit Tip

Think in terms of seeking to harvest the whitetail in their kitchen and not their bedroom.

DEEPER WOODS
DAY 17

The Harvest

Do not be deceived, God is not mocked; for whatever a man sows, this he will also reap. Let us not lose heart in doing good, for in due time we will reap if we do not grow weary.
Galatians 6:7,9

One of the most painstaking, yet rewarding, phases of preseason preparation is planting food plots. Hunters in the Southeast get to experience a true taste of all four seasons. This allows crop growth for deer to eat well, both into the spring and fall. Having these plots especially in the winter months, provide deer with a constant source of vital nutrition. Furthermore, just as planting food plots can provide a staple to a deer's diet, it also rewards the hunter in seeing more deer and harvesting them. This concept can prove to be significant in our lives as well.

The scripture above states, "Do not be deceived, God is not mocked; for whatever a man sows, this he will also reap." God has placed laws within this world that govern it's processes, and one of those is the law of sowing and reaping. This does not mean that giving a $100 in the church offering plate today will yield $1,000 return next week. However, it does mean that God has His way of sending his blessing, favor and graces in special ways for those who seek to operate under the laws of sowing and reaping.

Whether it's being generous with your material blessings or generous with your kindness towards others, our heavenly Father loves to find ways of producing a harvest of return, especially to those who belong to Him.

Pursuit Tip

Make it a habit to walk your property frequently in the off season, so you can see potential lanes for the next season. Even properties you have hunted for years have new discoveries waiting to be found.

DEEPER WOODS
DAY 18

The Fall

How you have fallen from heaven, O star of the morning, son of the dawn! You have been cut down to the earth, You who have weakened the nations!
Isaiah 14:12

One fall evening, as I was making my way down from a friend's Summit climber, the bottom suddenly fell out! If you have never "been there and done that," you have only missed something short of a heart attack! In short order, I was clinging to that tree like a firefighter to his pole, shimmying down with a cat-like grip! It was an intense moment to say the least.

Countless hunting accidents can be attributed to a fall. While some are more life threatening than others, all of them have two common denominators: each accident has a reason and each is dangerous, if not deadly. The same can be said of the falls in our lives.

If you're like me, you have experienced a fall in life and not just one or two but many! And no, I'm not talking about a physical fall, but a spiritual fall that results from a bad choice or decision. The Bible is crystal clear on the primary reason these types of falls often occur. It can be summed up and packaged into one word- PRIDE. In fact, the Bible tells us in Proverbs 16:18, that pride goes before the fall. Pride is that monster that often feeds our ego and makes us believe we can be and act independently from God. In fact, the scriptures tell us that it was exactly this venom that got Satan kicked out of heaven when he boasted, "I will make myself like the Most High (Isaiah 14:14)."

If there is one thing I have learned in this life, it is this truth: "God is opposed to the proud, but gives grace to the humble (James 4:6)." Jesus said, "Whoever exalts himself shall be humbled; and whoever humbles himself shall be exalted (Matthew 23:12)."

So whether it's retelling a hunt of a lifetime, or it's having the proper heart posture of humility before Almighty God in every area of life, may we always seek to promote humility over pride.

Pursuit Tip

Practice does not make perfect; perfect practice does. Never devalue the need for target practice. It can be the difference in wounding an animal or missing a trophy altogether.

DEEPER WOODS
DAY 19

The Cross Hairs

Search me, O God, and know my heart; try me and know my anxious thoughts. And see if there be any hurtful way in me, and lead me in the everlasting way.
Psalm 139:23-24

Nikon, Bushnell, Luepold, Burris and Redfield, to name a few, are all popular scopes designed to magnify the hunter's sight. These enable the hunter to see close up in ways the naked eye does not allow.

The psalmist wrote in Psalm 139:23, "Search me, O God, and know my heart; try me and know my anxious thoughts. And see if there be any hurtful way in me, and lead me in the everlasting way." Did you catch that? What courage it takes for a man to possess this gut-wrenching honesty to ask his God to search him, and to ask if the perfect sight of the all-knowing Creator sees anything painful or hurtful coming from the creation.

Much like scopes enhance our ability to bring things we otherwise might not see into full view, allowing God's presence into our lives can do the same. Asking for his Spirit to search us on a daily basis by bringing hurtful and sinful ways into the cross-hairs of his sight, and allowing the shot of grace to ring out into these areas, are a must for the sincere follower of Christ.

Pursuit Tip
Some stand and spot locations are better in the late season rather than early and vice versa. Do not be overly discouraged if you don't see deer in a certain spot a few times. Remember, it only takes a second for one to step out!

DEEPER WOODS
DAY 20

Seeing the Unseen

For we walk by faith, not by sight
2 Corinthians 5:7

When I think about hunting, I think about the amount of faith that is required in the sport. In Hebrews 11:1, the Bible describes faith as being sure of what we hope for and certain of what we cannot see. When we go to our best places hoping to see what we have not seen, we are exercising a degree of faith in the field of hunting. The signs are often hopeful indicators that our faith will become sight for that which we are hunting.

The same can be said about our spiritual lives. Although we have not seen physical proof of the eternity spoken of in the Bible, we see the evidence of the Creator's handiwork pointing of to the existence of Heaven. The book of Romans states, "For since the creation of the world His invisible attributes, His eternal power and divine nature, have been clearly seen, being understood through what has been made, so that they are without excuse (Romans 1:20)."

Many have said if God would only show me a sign, then I would believe Him. The truth is—God already has shown us. Not only revealed through nature but also through the person of Jesus Christ. God has revealed Himself to all humanity offering his ultimate sign of love on the cross as he bore for the forgiveness of our sins. When we receive this forgiveness offered by faith, we then gain the hope that one day our faith will become sight when we see Him face to face.

Pursuit Tip
Keep ya eyes up and ears open when walking to and from deer stands. Many opportunities can present themselves in these moments.

DEEPER WOODS
DAY 21

The Man Gods Uses

...they were uneducated and untrained men, they were amazed, and began to recognize them as having been with Jesus.
Acts 4:13

On Oct. 27, 2016, my phone rang at approximately 8:30 a.m. I recall the date because our ministry was headed to Cleveland, Ohio, where we would lead a missions team for the weekend. I looked at my phone, saw who was calling, and thought to myself -- he has a story to tell!

I answer the phone not with the common hello, but with the, "did you kill the 'biggun'"? Where I come from on the east coast in South Carolina we say 'biggun' and not 'big one'! Well, he proceeds to tell me he and his buddy were on the road to a job for work when they came upon an accident. A small Honda Civic had hit a deer and somehow flipped over on the deer, trapping it and leaving it severely wounded. They were able to move the car up enough to allow the deer to limp out through a nearby cut over, but the plot thickens!

My buddy realizes the deer is getting away and will most likely endure suffering, either in the grips of coyotes or a slow bleeding out. He follows the deer and after a short chase, catches him and wrestles him to the ground. Next, he pulls out his knife and proceeds to slit the deer's throat. With great empathy for the deer in this difficult task, he covers the deer's eyes with his free hand and assures him it will be ok! Now, if that isn't a hunt, I don't know what is!

I want to turn my man card and hunting license in when I think about this story! I am thoroughly convinced that I am not the expert hunter among us. Yes, I have written and published this devotional book for hunters, but at the risk of disappointing anyone, there are many whose experience and success in the outdoors far outweigh mine. Nonetheless, it does not subtract from the privilege and pursuit we enjoy, although we may sometimes feel that our expertise is less than others.

I am reminded of the men and women God uses for His purposes. They do not have to be the smartest, wealthiest, tallest or even the most popular to be used by God. They simply need to be available. When we look at those Jesus first called to be his disciples, we know that they were untrained and uneducated men. They were the fishermen of the day -- common folk, like most of us. And these eleven men were used, as the scriptures state, to turn the world upside down! The common fact that made these men uncommon was that they had been with Jesus. That is what qualified them for the mission!

Think about your life. What could God begin to do through you, if you made yourself fully available and obedient to His call of spending time with Him on a regular basis? Perhaps by being with Him, He would lead you to take an overseas missions trip and allow you to see the world through his eyes by helping many who are less fortunate. Maybe he has blessed you in such a way that by spending time with him, you begin to realize how you are able to leverage your talents and or resources for the glory of his mission.

Regardless, of how big or small we think our contribution may be to the kingdom, we can all be assured that in God's economy, the measuring stick for success over the centuries has been those whose hearts are found to be fully devoted to His.

Pursuit Tip
Deer know the smells of the woods better than any. Sometimes our unconscious habits can hinder the areas deer frequent.

DEEPER WOODS
DAY 22

A Friend Closer Than A Brother

But there is a friend who sticks closer than a brother.
Proverbs 18:24

It was the last day of an awesome season. I had just returned home from what would be the final hunt of the year. I'll admit, I was kind of bummed as I took the camo off for the last time and settled down into the recliner to warm up from the damp and cold rain that had moved in that evening.

When you devote all the passion you have into the game each season, you have that reflection moment. That moment of recalling all the good times, let downs and disappointments of the countless hours that have accompanied the season's pursuit.

Just as I settled into the recliner, the phone rang. A long-time friend of mine had called to tell me he had shot a deer early in the hunt. He had waited to near dark to begin the trackng, believing it was nearby, only to discover it was not. He needed a friend and his dog. Oh man, the season suddenly came back to life! It wasn't quite over just yet!

It didn't matter that I was forty minutes out from the location. It didn't matter that the temperature was dropping, and the solid flow of rain was soaking down. I had a friend that was in need of my help, and that's all that mattered.

We are blessed in this life to get to enjoy some fantastic relationships within the brotherhood of hunting. It's a family affair that can be picked back up, right where it left off. It's a connection that crosses all states and has no borders. Considering my hunting brotherhood reminds me of the similarities with the friend who is able to stick closer than a brother.

He is the One -- when our backs are up against the wall – who will indeed have our backs. He is the One -- when all others are unfaithful – who remains faithful with His steadfast love. He is the One -- When all that we know suddenly changes – who is constant and never changes. It is in the very heart and nature of God to show Himself dependable in ways such as the psalmist who had come to know Him. This is aptly described when He penned, "God is our refuge and strength, A very present help in trouble" (Psalm 46:1). And it is in this, that we too can trust Him as being a friend that will never leave us nor forsake us. Give Him a call today, He's there waiting to answer!

Pursuit Tip
Mineral blocks in the off season are a great way to provide deer herds the vital nutrients for health and maximum antler growth.

DEEPER WOODS
DAY 23

Frustrating Circumstances

For our light and momentary troubles are achieving for us an eternal glory that far outweighs them all.
2 Corinthians 4:17(NIV)

Hunting whitetail with a bow is a whole other world. The movement necessary to execute a full-draw under the stealth of cover, accompanied with hair-like precision, is nothing short of an art. Seeing an arrow soar towards it's target is unlike anything -- else and so are it's frustrations! Arrows falling out of their quiver, bows clinging to stands and rope becoming tangled, will not only make your blood pressure rise, it will also make the hunter wonder, 'why in the world do I enjoy this?' It takes you to the highest of highs and brings you to the lowest of lows.

It amazes me when reflecting on bow hunting, or hunting in general, how the frustrations can sometimes rise to a level where we will call into question the passions we pursue. It is in these moments that we are pushed to consider 'the why' and reasoning behind what we do. I call this, a soul check. When the kids don't make the best decisions they were taught, when we take one step forward and two steps back, our frustrations mount. Simply put, we all are faced with the frustrating circumstances that make up this thing called life.

It is moments like these, we are called to reflect on our purpose and calling. We have to consider the big picture in that hardships, setbacks and frustrations can all be the processes God uses to shape us into the person He is calling us to be. In fact, scriptures highlight this concept when saying, "For our light and momentary troubles are achieving for us an eternal glory that far outweighs them all (Romans 5:3-4 NIV)."

If you are like me, and most likely every other person who has ever lived, you enjoy it when things go good. This is why we need to often be reminded that there are reasons behind the struggles we go through, and that we should embrace these processes as a part of the different seasons of life.

Pursuit Tip

Practice your bow hunting shots from elevated heights. This will best prepare you for most realistic angles that most stands often present.

DEEPER WOODS
DAY 24

Persistence

Yet those who wait for the LORD Will gain new strength; They will mount up with wings like eagles, They will run and not get tired, They will walk and not become weary.
Isaiah 40:31

New properties can present new challenges. I gained rights to hunt a small 100 acre tract that had a three acre pond sitting at the back of it. The back access road that ran across the dam and over to the other side was flooded from beaver dams. I worked religiously tearing out and tearing down, wading in the waters to allow water to run smoothly out the back spillway. As sure as I would tear debris, limbs and grass out, I would come back only to find the beavers had built it back over night. This process went on for months! Their persistence was testing mine to the point where eliminating the beavers was the only way to eliminate the problem.

Have you ever had a hurdle in front of you or a challenge that you knew was not going to go away quickly or easily? Have you ever felt that perhaps the strength you possessed was not the strength needed for the obstacle? Life sometimes has it's way of doing that to us. If there is anything I have learned from my time spent on this earth, it's this truth: many circumstances arise where I need the strength and persistence mentioned by Isaiah the prophet when he wrote, "Yet those who wait for the LORD Will gain new strength; They will mount up with wings like eagles, They will run and not get tired, They will walk and not become weary (Isaiah 40:31)."

Notice the author's response to his trial. He didn't run ahead of God and try to fix it on his on. He didn't google a solution or watch a how- to video on you tube. He simply waited. It is in the waiting-on-God moments of our lives, that he makes us stronger and grants us the persistence needed to face them. It is in the waiting that we learn to gain new strength to run and not get tired, to walk and not grow weary. It is in these moments that we can gain the strength and persistence necessary to soar like wings of eagles over whatever the circumstances of life may throw at us.

Pursuit Tip
Planting fruit trees on a property can serve as a hotspot for a deer's nutrition. Consider it the dessert bar for the whitetail world.

DEEPER WOODS
DAY 25

Within Range

Test yourselves to see if you are in the faith; examine yourselves! Or do you not recognize this about yourselves, that Jesus Christ is in you—unless indeed you fail the test?
2 Corinthians 13:5

A successful hunt can come down to a matter of inches when trying to ensure a proper shot placement, especially when the bow is in hand. Twenty-three yards from the base or thirty-two yards from the height of the tree to be exact! This is where knowing and examining the exact range of a deer's distance can serve vital between the difference of life and death towards the hunter's success.

Just as range finders examine exact distances between target and hunter, the Bible exhorts hunters of the faith to do the same. The Bible states, "Test yourselves to see if you are in the faith; examine yourselves! Or do you not recognize this about yourselves, that Jesus Christ is in you—unless indeed you fail the test (2 Corinthians 13:5)?"

Securing a successful kill knows no limit with the avid hunter. The same should ring true from the imperative given from the apostle Paul to the church stationed in Corinth. Examining ourselves to ensure we are of the faith is paramount and carries with it the implications of life or death.

Billy Graham, who has preached face to face to more people on planet earth than anyone, had this to say about those who potentially call themselves followers of the faith. He states that he estimates 80% of those who attend church services are not actually born again followers of Jesus. This is where testing and examining one's self is paramount in ensuring we are able to go deeper in our faith.

Jesus stated in John 15 you can judge a tree by its fruit: no bad tree produces good fruit and no good tree produces bad fruit. The true test of marksmanship as a follower of Christ can be seen clearly when we come into the range of God's presence towards our hearts, allowing us to see whether Christ resides there through the Holy Spirit.

It has been said that twelve inches is all that separates a person from heaven or hell, meaning that it is twelve inches from a person's head to their heart. Professing Christ is much different than possessing Christ. Similar to how inches can mean the difference in the world of hunting, the same can be said of eternity.

Are you of the Faith?
Have you Passed the Test?

Pursuit Tip

Corn piles, as we like to call them in the South, are a great way to take inventory of the bucks on properties and to keep the does fat and happy!

DEEPER WOODS
DAY 26

Faith That Works

Even so faith, if it has no works, is dead being by itself
James 2:17

What if all we as hunters ever did was talk about hunting but we never actually got around to going hunting? We cleaned our guns, built a nice huge condo stand, scent controlled our clothes, read articles about other people hunting and the best tips of the trade, but we never actually went hunting for ourselves. Many perhaps would question how well of a hunter we actually were.

Many times our faith can carry these same parallels if we aren't careful. What benefit would it be to say we have faith but never discover what it means to truly serve others. To not only see those who need a lifting but being willing to be the means by which they are lifted. To enter into the lives of those who cannot in return do anything for us is what it means for us to pull the trigger towards both that of both faith and works. It is when these two expressions collide that the world will know that we are disciples of Jesus by the love we have love one to another.

Pursuit Tip

People often think the rut is the best time to kill big ones. Consider a prime time being while the bucks are still in their summer patterns. You can have a five-year-old buck down to the minute he's coming out. After he sheds the velvet, he's a different animal.

DEEPER WOODS
DAY 27

Lessons Learned

All discipline for the moment seems not to be joyful, but sorrowful; yet to those who have been trained by it, afterwards it yields the peaceful fruit of righteousness.
Hebrews 12:11

I know most of you reading aren't like me. You never have pulled off on a shot only to watch the deer you just missed stare back at you. You probably never have dropped your cell phone, cup, hat or anything else from the deer stand only to hear it sounding like it echoed across the county lines. Or perhaps my favorite – you probably have never driven out to your spot only to realize you left the gun, ammo or other necessity behind!

If I'm honest, I have made my fair share of mistakes in the world of hunting. But what I have learned is that mistakes have often led to my growth as a hunter. It's taken me getting busted from the wind to truly learn the importance the windage plays towards my potential success. It's taken the stress of my mess to help produce my success.

The same has also been found to be true in my walk with Jesus. I have made my fair share of mistakes when trying to live for him. Well, ok I have made a ton of mistakes in this pursuit. But here is the great reveal that I have learned. The scriptures have come alive that read "All discipline for the moment seems not to be joyful, but sorrowful; yet to those who have been trained by it, afterwards it yields the peaceful fruit of righteousness (Hebrews 12:11)." In the many times I have failed the Savior, I have learned His discipline leads to my betterment. He uses his discipline in our lives to shape and mold us into his image -- to create a righteousness within us, that otherwise wouldn't be possible. When we yield to these lessons learned from our mistakes, we gain the valuable training necessary to achieve the peaceful fruit of righteousness that comes into our lives as its result.

Pursuit Tip

Pay close attention to the weather patterns and forecasts. Hunting prior to or right after weather fronts move through can pay big dividends when hunting whitetails.

DEEPER WOODS
DAY 28

The Investment

The things which you have heard from me in the presence of many witnesses, entrust these to faithful men who will be able to teach others also.
2 Timothy 2:2

Most hunters have experienced the delight that comes from investing in the less experienced younger hunters. Whether it's a father showing his child the ropes or the club opening it's stands for a youth hunt, the investment and joy that come with passing down the tips of the trade certainly have their lasting rewards. There is a stark comparison to the process of teaching and modeling before the younger eyes to follow. This correlation can be observed in our primary call to be hunters of men.

I agree with the concept that life is caught rather than taught. This is also a form of teaching. Our primary call, as followers of Christ, is to teach those we have been entrusted with the lessons of life and the scriptures. This is called discipleship. Simply put, it's teaching someone to follow you as you follow someone, namely Jesus.

It is not easy but the call is clear. The results are not usually instant but always lasting. It takes time and a commitment to the long haul. It takes an intentional effort to invest in those God has placed around us. A son, a daughter, a grandson, nephew or friend of a friend are all examples of those God has presented to us for this beautiful opportunity to fulfill what Paul spelled out to Timothy when he wrote, "The things which you have heard from me in the presence of many witnesses, entrust these to faithful men who will be able to teach others also (2 Timothy 2:2)." When we express this simple, but important, command of Jesus to make disciples, we become a lasting investment of God's ways to future generations.

Pursuit Tip

Deer love nothing more than natural food sources in abundance. Find such food sources as white oaks, and you will find your deer.

DEEPER WOODS
DAY 29

The Warden

For the word of the LORD is right and true; he is faithful in all he does.
Psalm 33:4 (NIV)

The Bible says confession is good for the soul. It's also humbling! While on the road traveling much of one summer, I worked hard to run game cameras and prep the hunting land. My best access to the upcoming season's rule book was looking online using my phone. I was certain I was clear about the first day of doe season, even verifying with other outdoorsman. As it drew closer, a ministerial friend contacted me asking could we hunt together as he needed some meat in the freezer for his family. With deer still walking in their summer patterns, I was sure I had just the spot!

I dropped him off at the tripod stand overlooking the backside of a pasture. I went down about 300 yards, where I would be looking at the neck of the same area. Earlier than expected, I had two does step out 60 yards in front of me. Always being anxiously excited to pull the trigger early in the season and get that first one in the books, I did so and she dropped like a sack of potatoes. I was hoping it was just a matter of time before my pal did the same.

Finally, with last light fleeting, my friend hunkered down on what would be a nice doe for himself. We were thrilled that we had doubled down on what we *thought* was opening day of doe season for our zone. As I often do, I shared the joy of our hunt on social media. This is when it got quite interesting. Guys started posting that it was an illegal harvest. I was certain of what I had read and had a screen shot of the online page. I started contacting other friends asking if I had been wrong? Some said yes, some no!

Thanks to all the "Davey Crocketts" of the social media world, that next afternoon during lunch, I watched as two green DNR trucks came rolling up the driveway. They got out and after the cordial introduction asked me the million dollar question -- did it happen? I said, "Yes sir." I then showed one of them the hardcopy of the DNR's rule book, which clearly stated we were in the good. The problem came when the previous page stated the contrary. One officer commented stating, "I see how that can be confusing." However, the officers didn't seem confused when they issued me a nice ticket before they left.

One clear takeaway from the adventurous event that often relates to our lives in general, is the truth that, "There is a way that seems right to a man, but its end is the way of death (Proverbs 16:25)." Often times we think ourselves to be striving and following the right path. We believe our decisions to be the best decisions. Whether it's career moves or child raising, we need to understand and embrace the reality that even at our best, we stand in need of guidance. This is another reason we seek to trust God's Book as our guide. It's been said the acronym for the Bible could be seen as:

Basic
Instructions
Before
Leaving
Earth

God's Word has stood the test of time. Kings have ruled by it and kings have fallen by it. When we choose to humbly embrace it's leadership in our lives by diving into it on a regular basis, we are then able to see life's clear path calling out saying, "This is the way, walk in it (Isaiah 30:21)."

Pursuit Tip

Always ask questions from other hunters. It's amazing what you can pick up and apply to your own personal bag of tricks!

DEEPER WOODS
DAY 30

The Right Way

Therefore, to one who knows the right thing to do and does not do it, to him it is sin.
James 4:17

I don't always like it. Heck, sometimes I seem to despise it. But nonetheless, I still do it. I am talking about those hunts when I just don't feel like hunting. When the season has been long and the temperatures are colder than usual, I must confess the warm bed is much more appealing.

While there are times that I succumb to sleeping in during the season, there also as many times that I don't. If I had a dollar for every time I hunted when I did not feel like it, I could probably be a rich man! Besides, as one friend put it, 'The good Lord only give us so many days in a year to kill them!'

There are many a hunter in whom I'm sure can say the same, who on the occasions when they don't feel like hunting, press on because of their passion and desire for the game.

This same parallel can be said of followers of Christ. Doing the right thing even when we don't feel like it is to be the Christian's pursuit. It is in this pursuit we find ourselves serving others even at a personal cost to ourselves. Like a good hunting routine, we find ourselves as followers of Christ committed to the routine of spiritual disciplines -- disciplines such as the personal reading of God's Word and the gathering with other believers on a consistent basis. These gatherings encourage us with the Word, causing iron to sharpen iron as we forge ahead together in the journey to know Him better.

When it's all said and done, there will often be those moments in our faith journey that we will want to sleep in. When these moments come, as they will, may we be reminded of the great prize that awaits all those who are faithful to the end of life's season here on this earth. The prize of hearing the words "Well done, good and faithful servant (Matthew 25:23 NIV)."

Pursuit Tip

Look for crossings on nearby creek banks when considering stand locations. Deer like to use the same crossings when frequenting certain areas.

DEEPER WOODS
DAY 31

The Final Hunt

"For the Son of Man has come to seek and to save that which was lost."
Luke 19:10

In October 1999, the greatest hunt of my life came to an end -- that morning, God found me. See, for the first 17 years of my life, pride and rebellion kept me from God's desire to have a personal relationship with me through his Son, the Lord Jesus Christ. I always believed there was a God and was even well versed in the, "now I lay me down to sleep, I pray the Lord my soul to keep" prayer. However, I didn't know God in the personal way the Bible talks about. Because my sins and heart of stone stood in need of the softening graces of Jesus, I was separated from Him.

I went to church that morning with the intention of giving God "a try" - a last resort before I would simply decide to perhaps end it all. I even sat at the end of the pew that morning to make the trip to the altar easier. Sure enough, during the invitation that Sunday morning, God met me where I was. As the old hymn "I Surrender All" played, I surrendered all to the Jesus who had hunted me for all those years.

We sometimes don't like to admit it as hunters, but if we are all honest, we all stand in need of help. While we all come from different backgrounds, experiences and walks of life, we still all share the same common denominator -- the need to say yes to Jesus. This is not a yes to church membership, a dunk or sprinkle in baptism, or even giving money to the Little League team because it makes you feel good. No, this is a moment in time - a definite time and place, followed by a continual obedience of laying our 'yes' on God's table of complete surrender.

The Bible declares that, "For all have sinned and fallen short of the glory of God (Romans 3:23)." This means that all of us have missed the mark of hitting God's bull's eye or standard of perfection seen in the Ten Commandments. Furthermore, the Bible states, " The wages of sin is death, (Romans 6:23)." This is both a spiritual death and physical death. Physical death separates us from this earth, and spiritual death separates us from the eternity spent with God in heaven and leads us to the place called Hell. If a person chooses to never to turn from their sins and place by their total, by faith, in God's only begotten Son, the Bible is clear of their fate. While this bad news is no respecter of persons, there is good news that follows: "God demonstrates his own love towards us, in that while we were yet sinners, Christ died for us (Romans 5:8)." The good news has no end "The free gift of God is eternal life in Christ Jesus Christ our Lord (Romans 6:23)."

It has been this free gift that has turned my world upside down for the better. It not only has given me the promise of my eternal home in the near future, it has given me a power and purpose to live in today.

There are many reading this who have experienced this unspeakable gift.

And there are many who simply have not. If you have not, I urge you to realize that today is the day of salvation. Let this day be the day you lay your 'yes' on God's table of complete surrender. Let today be the day that God's hunt in your life comes to an end, and let it be the day you are hunted and helped for His glory and your greater good.

Dear Jesus, I simply ask you to forgive me for all my sins. I believe you died on the cross for my sins and rose again on the third day. By faith, I receive you into my life and ask from this day forward that you be my guide, my master and my Lord. Thank you for hearing my prayer. It's in Jesus's Name I pray. Amen

Pursuit Tip

The deer will never surrender because it only leads to death. A man's surrender leads to abundant life.

ABOUT THE AUTHOR

Michael Anderson is Founder and Executive Director of All For One Ministries and lead pastor of All For One Church. He has been the keynote speaker for wild-game dinners and his travels have taken him to five continents and more than a dozen countries. If he isn't circling the globe sharing the life-changing message of Jesus Christ that changed his life nearly 18 years ago, you can find him in a deer stand stalking a southern whitetail or on the water fishing. He is a graduate of Wingate University with a major in Religious Studies and minor in psychology. He earned his Master of Divinity degree from Columbia International University in Ministry Leadership.

To learn more about Michael and All For One Ministries or to have him come speak at your event you can visit the website www.allofusforone.org

ON DECEMEBER 11ᵀᴴ 2017 THE LORD BLESSED BY ALLOWING ME TO TAKE THE BOOKS COVER DEER AFFECTIONATELY NAMED, DONKEY KONG.

AS THE DEER PANTS FOR THE WATER BROOKS, SO MY SOUL PANTS FOR YOU, O GOD.
PSALM 42:1

Made in the USA
Columbia, SC
11 September 2019